Centered on Learning
SPRING

Over 90 Terrific Seasonal Center Ideas

Table of Contents

1

More learning center books from *The Mailbox®*

Project Editors: Cindy K. Daoust, Angie Kutzer, Jan Trautman
Copy Editors: Gina Farago, Karen Brewer Grossman, Karen L. Huffman,
   Amy Kirtley, Debbie Shoffner
Cover Artists: Kimberly Richard, Nick Greenwood
Art Coordinator: Rebecca Saunders
Artists: Pam Crane, Teresa R. Davidson, Theresa Lewis Goode, Nick Greenwood,
   Sheila Krill, Clint Moore, Rebecca Saunders, Barry Slate, Donna K. Teal
Typesetters: Lynette Maxwell, Mark Rainey

President, The Mailbox Book Company™: Joseph C. Bucci
Book Development Managers: Stephen Levy, Elizabeth H. Lindsay,
   Thad McLaurin, Susan Walker
Book Planning Manager: Chris Poindexter
Curriculum Director: Karen P. Shelton
Traffic Manager: Lisa K. Pitts
Librarian: Dorothy C. McKinney
Editorial and Freelance Management: Karen A. Brudnak
Editorial Training: Irving P. Crump
Editorial Assistants: Terrie Head, Melissa B. Montanez, Hope Rodgers,
   Jan E. Witcher

www.themailbox.com

Manufactured in the United States
10 9 8 7 6 5 4 3 2 1

About This Book

Focus on fun and learning when you stock your classroom centers with the activities found in *Centered on Learning—Spring*. Just turn the page to find a fresh collection of 15 popular early childhood themes packed with activities for many of your most common learning centers. Each thematic unit includes

▶ Ideas and skills that are easily scanned, so you can choose the centers you need based on your students' needs

▶ All-new center ideas that reinforce curriculum concepts and skills

▶ Independent and small-group learning activities

▶ Ideas to help coordinate your centers with your current topics of study

Centered on Learning—Spring helps make planning simple, too! Since many of the units correspond to themes you already teach, all you need to do is scan the skills in each unit and then make your center selections. So use *Centered on Learning—Spring* to make the most of your valuable time and your classroom learning center opportunities!

3

Birds

Nestle these bird-related centers in your classroom to hatch some high-flying learning fun!

by Suzanne Moore

Little Bird's Color Words

Literacy Center

▶ colors
▶ color words
▶ oral language

Where does Little Bird belong? Your students will find out! In advance, copy the bird patterns (page 7) on white construction paper to make a set of eight birds. Color each bird a different color; then laminate all the patterns. (If desired, use a permanent marker to program each bird with its corresponding color word.) Next, label each of eight plastic tubs with a different color word. Fill each tub with Easter grass or raffia to resemble a bird's nest. To do this activity, encourage a child to say the rhyme below as he places each bird in its corresponding nest.

Little Bird, Little Bird, what's your color word?
Little Bird, Little Bird, you are (yellow)!

Adding Eggs

Math Center

▶ counting
▶ numeral recognition
▶ addition

Count on these colorful bird eggs to help your youngsters build their math skills. To prepare, make a nest by filling a plastic tub with raffia. Program a supply of sentence strips with simple addition problems. Cut off the end of each strip and write the corresponding sum on that section of the strip. (For self-checking purposes, program the back of each problem strip and sum strip with identical shapes. See note below.) Arrange the nest and strips in your math center along with a basket of colorful plastic eggs. To do this activity, instruct a child to choose a problem strip. Encourage him to place the eggs in the nest according to the addends in the problem. Have him count the total number of eggs and then select the strip that shows the correct sum. To check his work, have the child flip the strips and look for matching shapes.

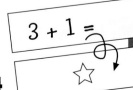

$2 + 1 =$

3

$3 + 1 =$

4

Note: If you use several problems that have the same sum (for example, 1 + 3 and 2 + 2), be sure to program the back of each strip involved with the *same* shape.

Seeds All Around

Little hands and fingers will love the unique experiences prompted by this center. In advance, pour a bag of mixed birdseed into a sensory tub. Provide measuring cups and spoons, a variety of bowls, and funnels. Encourage children who visit the center to run their hands through the seeds as they measure, pour, funnel, and creatively explore. When you're done with this center in your classroom, use the seed to feed the birds in your schoolyard!

Sensory Center

tactile experience ◄
fine-motor skills ◄
experience with ◄
capacity

Bird-Watching

Take flight into bird research with this child-centered research area. First, designate an area of your classroom (or playground) to be the bird-watching center. Stock the area with paper, pencils, crayons, and a pair of binoculars. Also provide a variety of bird books (see the list below). Invite your students to observe birds from the bird-watching area and examine the books in the center. Encourage each child to record her observations by writing and/ or drawing. Then have each child share her findings with the class. Afterward, bind each child's research page into a class book titled "Bird-Watching."

Discovery Center

fine-motor skills ◄
investigation ◄
recording ◄
information

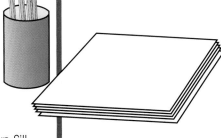

Leigh

A bird can jump.

About Birds: A Guide for Children by Cathryn Sill
Bird (Eyewitness Books) by David Burnie
Outside and Inside Birds by Sandra Markle
Unbeatable Beaks by Stephen R. Swinburne

Bird's Buffet

These tasty treats are *definitely* for the birds! Arrange the supplies (from the list below) for easy student access. Have each child who visits the center spread a thin coat of peanut butter on the cut side of a bagel half. Then instruct him to press the bagel into the birdseed. After he removes the bagel from the seed, help him tie a length of ribbon through the hole. Have each child store his project in a resealable plastic bag. Invite each child to take his project home and find a place to perch his buffet for the birds around his house.

You will need:
a class supply of bagel halves
a class supply of 14"–18" ribbons
peanut butter
plastic knives
a shallow pan of birdseed
paper towels or napkins
a class supply of resealable
    plastic bags

Cooking Center

▶ *fine-motor skills*
▶ *following directions*

Build a Bird

Originality flies high with this creative art activity. To prepare, cut out a variety of colorful construction paper shapes (refer to the illustration for ideas). Put the shapes in your art center along with some glue sticks, wiggle eyes, craft feathers, scissors, and crayons. Encourage each child to use the supplies as she likes to create her own original bird or birds. Mount the completed projects on a bulletin board. If desired, post a speech balloon near each bird and record each artist's dictation about her bird.

Art Center

▶ *fine-motor skills*
▶ *creative expression*
▶ *spatial awareness*

I am a penguin, which is a bird, too. by Jane

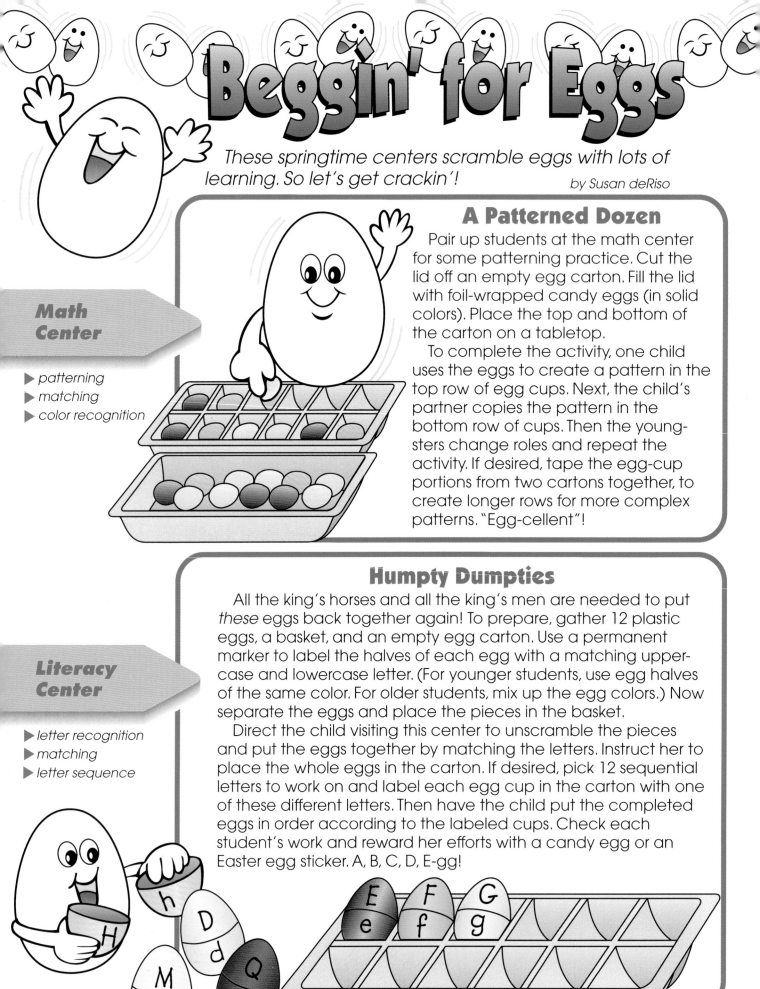

Beggin' for Eggs

These springtime centers scramble eggs with lots of learning. So let's get crackin'!

by Susan deRiso

Math Center

▶ patterning
▶ matching
▶ color recognition

A Patterned Dozen

Pair up students at the math center for some patterning practice. Cut the lid off an empty egg carton. Fill the lid with foil-wrapped candy eggs (in solid colors). Place the top and bottom of the carton on a tabletop.

To complete the activity, one child uses the eggs to create a pattern in the top row of egg cups. Next, the child's partner copies the pattern in the bottom row of cups. Then the youngsters change roles and repeat the activity. If desired, tape the egg-cup portions from two cartons together, to create longer rows for more complex patterns. "Egg-cellent"!

Literacy Center

▶ letter recognition
▶ matching
▶ letter sequence

Humpty Dumpties

All the king's horses and all the king's men are needed to put *these* eggs back together again! To prepare, gather 12 plastic eggs, a basket, and an empty egg carton. Use a permanent marker to label the halves of each egg with a matching uppercase and lowercase letter. (For younger students, use egg halves of the same color. For older students, mix up the egg colors.) Now separate the eggs and place the pieces in the basket.

Direct the child visiting this center to unscramble the pieces and put the eggs together by matching the letters. Instruct her to place the whole eggs in the carton. If desired, pick 12 sequential letters to work on and label each egg cup in the carton with one of these different letters. Then have the child put the completed eggs in order according to the labeled cups. Check each student's work and reward her efforts with a candy egg or an Easter egg sticker. A, B, C, D, E-gg!

8

Egg Layers

Keep your youngsters guessing with this eggy game. To prepare, draw a simple gameboard on tagboard, similar to the one shown. Make a copy of the cards on page 11. Color the cards and then cut them apart on the dotted lines. Fold each card in half and tape the ends together. If desired, laminate the cards and gameboard.

To play the game, stack the cards with the animal sides faceup on the board. Give each of two players a game piece, such as a bingo chip or a seasonal counter. Have the first player identify the animal on top of the stack and guess whether it lays eggs. Then instruct the child to turn the card over to check his guess. If he is correct, he moves his game piece one space. If he is incorrect, play continues with the next player and the next card. Once all the cards are used, shuffle them and stack them faceup again. The game ends when one (or both) players reach the finish line.

Literacy
Center

critical thinking ◀
number ◀
sequence
taking turns ◀

How Do You Like 'Em?

Your sensory center is the perfect place for this egg-tasting graph. Arrange to have parent volunteers work with small groups of students to prepare two or three different egg dishes, such as deviled eggs, scrambled eggs, omelettes, quiche, French toast, or egg salad. Make a grid containing the names of the prepared foods. Have each child sample the foods and then color a block on the grid to indicate her favorite egg choice. Now it's time to "eggs-amine" the graph's results!

How Do You Like 'Em?

Deviled	Scrambled	French Toast

Sensory
Center

following ◀
directions
fine-motor skills ◀
sequencing steps ◀
exploring taste ◀
graphing ◀

- fine-motor skills
- creative expression
- color and texture exploration

Expressive Eggs

These unique keepsakes will turn givers' *and* receivers' faces sunnyside up. To prepare, cut out a tagboard egg shape for each child. On each egg, write the verse shown. Have each child sign his name on his egg below the verse. Then instruct him to turn his egg over and decorate it with a variety of craft items, such as sequins, ribbon, glitter, and dimensional paint. It's a gift that would make any mother hen proud!

Some eggs are green.
Some eggs are blue.
But this special egg
Was made just for you!
Love,
Ben

- counting down
- dramatic play
- rhyming

Cheep, Cheep!

Little fingers play a big part in this musical center. To prepare, cut apart the egg cups in an empty carton. Then trim the top of each cup to look like a cracked egg and cut an X in the bottom of each cup. Put a supply of the finished egg cups in your music center along with a pad of washable yellow ink.

Teach youngsters the song below during circle time. Then invite each child to visit the music center to dramatize the song. To do this, a child pushes an egg cup on each finger of one hand and then presses the end of each finger into the yellow ink to resemble a chick. As each chick goes to sleep, the child removes one egg cup and folds that finger down. Sweet dreams, you tired babies!

Five Baby Chicks
(sung to the tune of "Five Little Ducks")

(Five) baby chicks hatched out one day.
Inside their nest they wiggled away.
With a peck, peck and a cheep, cheep, cheep!
One little chick fell fast asleep.

*Repeat the verse for four, three, and two;
then sing the last verse (below).*

One baby chick hatched out one day.
Inside his nest he wiggled away.
With a peck, peck and a cheep, cheep, cheep!
No one to play with, I might as well sleep!

Farm Frolics!

Rise and shine! Head on down to the barn to feed some chickens, milk some cows, and practice some basic skills.

by Angie Kutzer and dayle timmons

Literacy Center

▶ *creative writing*
▶ *rhyming*
▶ *creative expression*

I'm in the Rhyme!

Give your youngsters a chance to be the stars of their own nursery rhymes. During a group time, review favorite rhymes that relate to the farm, such as "Little Boy Blue," "Little Bo-Peep," or "Mary Had a Little Lamb." Then choose a language chunk from each rhyme and demonstrate how to personalize it for a child in your class. For example, "(Justin) had a little (goat)." Post sections of the traditional rhymes in your literacy center with blank spaces as shown. Then invite each child to visit the center and write or dictate his own rhyme on a large sheet of art paper. Then invite him to illustrate his new creation. Bind all the rhymes together for a new class book. Read the book aloud during your next circle time; then put it in the reading center for individual reading.

Justin had a little goat.

[_____] had a little [_____].

Math Center

▶*number recognition*
▶*number sequence*
▶*one-to-one correspondence*

Gatherin' Eggs

It's off to the chicken coop to gather up some "egg-y" math skills. Use a permanent marker to label each of 12 Ping-Pong® balls (eggs) with a different number from 1 to 12. (For younger students, label the egg cups in an empty egg carton with the numbers 1 to 12 as well.) Store the eggs in a basket; then put the basket and empty egg carton in the math center. To complete the activity, invite an older child to put the eggs in numerical order and a younger student to match each egg to its corresponding egg cup.

Floating Feathers?

Gather your youngsters and have them brainstorm a list of animals that have feathers. Then have volunteers circle the animals on the list that are found on a farm. After the list is made, pass around real feathers or realistic-looking craft feathers. Encourage youngsters to give descriptive words as they examine the feathers. Then pose this question: "Do feathers float?" Prepare two simple T graphs. On one, direct each child to clip a personalized clothespin to the side that indicates her prediction.

Provide a supply of feathers and a tub of water in your science center. Hang the second T graph nearby. Have each child complete the experiment and clip a clothespin on the second graph to indicate her results. After center time, compare the predicted results against the actual results. Wow, how friends of a feather flock together!

Science Center

critical thinking ◀
predicting ◀
experimenting ◀

Here Chicky, Chicky!

Bang the pots and pans—it's feeding time! Explain to your little ones that a chicken's diet is made up mostly of corn. Show a few different examples of corn, such as popcorn kernels, popcorn, dried corn seed, and cornmeal. Then fill the sensory tub with actual chicken feed (for older students) or popcorn kernels (for younger students). Provide scoops, cups, and funnels for further exploration under adult supervision. Come and get it!

Sensory Center

exploration ◀
measurement ◀
fine-motor skills ◀

Art
Center

▶ *creative expression*
▶ *color exploration*
▶ *fine-motor skills*

"Udder-ly" Fun Art

Use rubber gloves to simulate milking a cow, and make some art in the process! After your students have experienced "milking" a cow, fill separate gloves with different colors of watered-down tempera paint. Knot each glove's opening; then poke a small hole in the ends of the gloves' index, middle, and ring fingers. Have each youngster use the gloves to squirt, drip, and drizzle paint designs onto a sheet of paper. Just "moo-velous!"

Motor
Center

▶ *fine-motor skills*
▶ *visual discrimination*
▶ *hand-eye coordination*

Sew and Sew

These cute lacing cards make practicing fine-motor skills a bushel of fun! To create the cards, duplicate the shapes on page 15 onto tagboard. Color the shapes, cut them out, and laminate them. Then use a hole puncher to make holes where indicated. Provide colorful shoestrings or lengths of yarn for youngsters to use to sew around the cards' edges. After a child has finished lacing, have him take out the shoestrings to ready the center for the next student. E-I-E-I-O!

RIBBIT!

Invite your little ones to jump into these frog centers, which are hopping with curriculum-related fun.

by Angie Kutzer and Mackie Rhodes

FLIPPING FROGS

Youngsters will jump at the chance to complete this counting activity. To prepare, make a supply of frog manipulatives from plastic jug lids. Simply stick a frog sticker to the top (flat side) of each lid. Next, cut out a large lily pad from bulletin board paper and tape it down to the floor.

Have each child thumb-flip (or toss) the frogs onto the lily pad from a designated distance. Then direct her to count how many frogs land faceup and how many land facedown. Have the child compare the two quantities and determine which amount is greater.

Math Center

▶ *counting*
▶ *comparing quantities*
▶ *fine-motor skills*

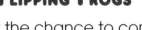

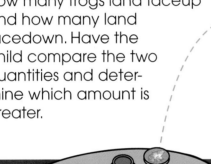

FROGS ON LOGS

Students exploring these magnetic frogs will discover that science is very attractive. Gather several miniature plastic or rubber frog figures. Hot-glue a magnet to the underside of each frog. Cut out a few lily pads from green card stock–weight paper.

Instruct a child to hold a magnet wand under the lily pad. Help him place a frog on top of the pad directly above the wand. Then have the child hold the lily pad with one hand and slowly move the wand with the other hand to manipulate the frog. Allow free exploration to see how many ways students find to move the frogs. It's an activity they're sure to stick with for a while!

Science Center

▶ *properties of magnets*
▶ *hand-eye coordination*
▶ *critical thinking*

LEAPING LILY PADS!

Hop into letter recognition and phonemic awareness skills with these linguistic lily pads. To prepare, cut a wedge out of each of five green paper plates. Program each plate with a different consonant: *d, f, h, j,* or *l.* Write the rime *-og* on a large index card. Spread the lily pads on the floor, post the card nearby, and provide a rubber frog toy or beanbag. To play, a child tosses the frog onto a lily pad. She then holds the designated lily pad next to the *-og* card, as shown, and reads the new word.

To adapt this idea for younger students, have children take turns tossing the frog and naming the letter (or giving its sound) on which the frog lands. They're learning by leaps and bounds!

Literacy Center

onsets and rimes ◀
letter recognition ◀
gross-motor skills ◀

IN THE POND

Create this unique pond where the only thing "whet" is youngsters' imaginations! Fill your sensory table with blue crinkled paper strips to represent water. Then add cardboard tube logs and craft foam lily pads. If possible, include a few dried cattails. Finally, gather a collection of frog toys—big ones, little ones, rubber ones, plastic ones, squeaky ones—and release them into this environment.

Invite visitors to the center to use the frogs to demonstrate positional concepts, such as *under* the water, *over* the lily pad, and *beside* the log. Then encourage students to play a quick game of hide-and-seek with the froggies. Be sure to also allow plenty of time just to let frogs be frogs!

Sensory Center

imaginative play ◀
exploring texture ◀
position words ◀

Art Center

▶ *creative expression*
▶ *fine-motor skills*
▶ *vocabulary development*

FROG FUN

Give busy little fingers a workout with these dotty frogs. Stock the art center with a supply of sticky dots, hole reinforcements, construction paper, scissors, and markers. Invite each child to use the materials to create frogs in different colors and poses. For more of a challenge, have the child write the action in which each frog is engaged. Ready, set, stick!

Cooking Center

▶ *following directions*
▶ *sequencing*
▶ *fine-motor skills*

FROG SNACKS

Getting a child to taste frog legs might be quite a feat, but you'll have no trouble at all convincing her to create and eat this funny frog. In advance, have a parent volunteer make a class supply of cupcakes without the icing. Duplicate the recipe cards on page 19. Color the cards and cut them apart. Post the cards in sequential order in your cooking center. Then arrange the ingredients and supplies listed below for easy student access. Invite each child to visit the center and follow the recipe cards to make a froggy snack.

Ingredients for one:
cupcake
green-tinted frosting
green candy fruit slice
2 chocolate chips
red Fruit Roll-Ups® piece (or licorice)

Utensils and supplies:
napkin (per child)
plastic knife (per child)

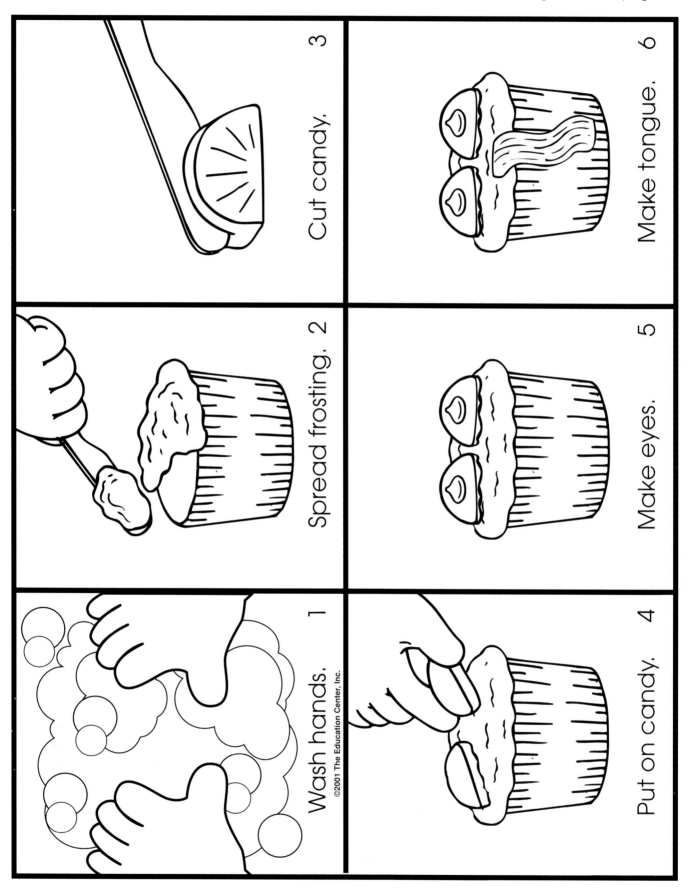

3

Cut candy.

6

Make tongue.

2

Spread frosting.

5

Make eyes.

1

Wash hands.

©2001 The Education Center, Inc.

4

Put on candy.

Flower Power

Bring your youngsters' skills into full bloom as they pick through this bouquet of centers.

by Melissa Hauck and Angie Kutzer

Literacy Center

▶ rhyming
▶ critical thinking
▶ vocabulary

Rhyming Roses

This file folder activity is a really rosy way to practice rhyming. To make the game, duplicate the rose and rosebud patterns (page 23) eight times onto red construction paper. Also make one copy of the picture cards (page 23). Cut out the flowers and cut apart the picture cards. For each rhyming pair of cards, glue one card onto a rose; then glue the matching card on a rosebud. Glue the roses on the inside of a green file folder. Laminate the folder. Stick the loop side of a Velcro® dot near each rose and the hook side of a Velcro dot on the back of each rosebud. Store the rosebuds in a zippered plastic bag taped to the back of the file folder.

To play, a child picks a rosebud, names the picture, and attaches the bud next to its rhyming rose. Reward efforts with a dollop of rose-scented hand lotion. Mmmm...lovely learning!

Math Center

▶ visual discrimination
▶ sorting
▶ fine-motor skills

All Sorts of Seeds

Help sorting skills take root in youngsters' minds with this activity. For younger students purchase three packs of flower seeds that look quite different. For older students buy more types of seeds or pick seeds that look similar. For each seed type, label a small paper plate with the flower's name, glue on a picture of the flower (can be cut out from seed package), and glue a few of the seeds to the plate. Mix up the remaining seeds and store them in a small flowerpot. Put the flowerpot, plates, and two pairs of tweezers in the math center. Then have pairs of students visit the center to sort the seeds. Let's get growing!

Four o'Clocks

Pansy Parts

What's got a stem, leaves, roots, and petals? A flowering plant, of course! Purchase a tray of pansies and place them in your discovery center along with several magnifying lenses, tweezers, and small gardening gloves (if desired). Invite each center visitor to explore the plants and identify their main parts. Engage students in a discussion about each plant part's specific job. For example, the roots absorb water and nutrients from the soil, and the stem supports and connects the other parts of the plant. Once every child has had a turn to investigate the pretty pansies, plant them in a window box for greater petal appeal!

Discovery Center

observing ◄
communicating ◄
vocabulary ◄

A Flower Shower

Use your water table to teach children how to properly water flowers. Explain that too much water too quickly could be damaging. Set up this exploration by moving your water table outside. Fill several flowerpots with sand and then insert artificial flowers into each pot. Provide watering cans, misting bottles, and paper cups (with different-sized holes in the bottoms) for youngsters to experiment with. Which containers allow for a slow and steady shower? After this experience, send a note to parents announcing that youngsters are ready to shower some flowers at home!

Sensory Center

fine-motor skills ◄
water exploration ◄
hand-eye ◄
coordination

A "Kinder-garden" Shop

This pretend flower shop provides students with many different opportunities for imaginative play. Fill a center with your choice of the props listed below. Then stand back and watch as your little sprouts grow into real entrepreneurs!

Possible props:

artificial flowers	tissue paper	gardening trowels	ribbon
seed packets	cash register	play money	notepads for orders
plastic flowerpots	telephone	price tags	plush toys
plastic vases	card picks	Mylar® balloons	gift cards
gloves	purses	on a stick	

Dramatic-Play Center

▶ role-playing
▶ verbal skills
▶ imaginative thinking

Mums for Mommies

These personalized flowers make great Mother's Day keepsakes. Cut large sheets of white construction paper in half to create long strips. Stock the art center with these paper strips, washable lavender or yellow paint, a paintbrush, green felt, scissors, glue, a green washable ink pad, markers, and a picture of each student. To create a flower, use a marker to make a small dot in the center of the paper toward the top. Have the student paint all four of his fingers on one hand and then make repeated prints around the dot, applying more paint as necessary. Allow the paint to dry. Then the student cuts a stem from green felt and glues it to the bottom of the flower. He makes green thumbprints along the stem to resemble leaves. Have him cut a photograph of himself into a circle and glue it in the center of the flower. Then he uses a marker to write "Thanks, Mom, for helping me grow!" and any other sentiments along the stem. Happy Mother's Day!

Art Center

▶ fine-motor skills
▶ printing technique
▶ craft project

rose

rosebud

picture cards

Bunnies!

Hippity-hop up to learning fun with these bunny center ideas!

by Roxanne LaBell Dearman

Bunny Bedtime

These little bunnies are hopping off to bed—in alphabet style! Use this adaptable center to address the needs of each of your children. To prepare, duplicate the bunny and basket patterns (page 27) on construction paper to make 26 of each. If desired, color the patterns; then laminate them. Use a permanent marker to write a different letter of the alphabet on each bunny and each basket. Adapt what each child will do in this center according to his abilities. For example, one child might match just five to ten bunnies to their baskets. Another child might put all the baskets in alphabetical order and match them up. Hippity-hop!

Literacy Center

▶ left-to-right progression
▶ letter recognition
▶ sequencing

Weighing Rabbit Food

Children will predict and verify which rabbit foods weigh the most, least, and just about the same. Put a variety of rabbit foods—such as carrots, green peppers, celery, broccoli, and lettuce—in a tub. Put the tub of foods in a center along with a balance scale. To do this activity, have a child select two different foods. Ask her to predict which food is heavier. Then have her use the balance scale to see for herself. If desired, ask each child to arrange the foods in order from lightest to heaviest.

Discovery Center

▶ tactile experience
▶ predicting
▶ weighing
▶ sequencing

24

Bunny Hops

Math skills hop right along with this fun activity! In advance, take photos of classroom destinations (such as your water fountain or bookshelf) or make simple drawings of them. Stock a center with the pictures and a supply of paper and pencils. Ask children to visit this center in pairs. Have one person choose a classroom destination card and estimate how many hops it will take him to get from the center to the destination and write down that guess. Then have the child who drew the card hop to the destination while his partner helps count the hops. Have the partner write down the actual number of hops. Then ask both partners to decide if the actual number was more than, less than, or equal to the estimated one. Then switch roles and continue in the same manner, hopping away!

Math Center

counting ◄
estimating ◄
measurement ◄
gross-motor skills ◄

Hide-and-Seek

Prepare your sensory center for a little gardening by adding potting soil, child-safe gardening tools, and plastic veggies and flowers. Invite your students to set up the garden as they work in pairs. Then have one child hide a plastic Peter Rabbit toy somewhere in the garden. Can the other child (Mr. MacGregor) find Peter? Have the children switch roles and play again, taking turns with the gardening chores.

Sensory Center

sensory experience ◄
visual discrimination ◄
fine-motor skills ◄

- *fine-motor skills*
- *creative expression*
- *spatial awareness*

Carrot Painting

Carrots are not only for eating! Try using them in your art center! Stock a center with all kinds of carrots: whole, round slices, diagonal slices, and vertically cut sticks. Also provide some art paper and orange tempera paint mixed with a few drops of dishwashing liquid. Invite your students to hop on over and experiment making prints and pictures. For added discovery, provide yellow and red paint and encourage children to see what happens as the colors mix together!

- *fine-motor skills*
- *following directions*
- *spatial awareness*

Bunny Tails

Tempt your youngsters with these delightful bunny tail snacks! Give each child a five-inch circular doily. Position a rice cake in the middle of the doily. Have each center visitor spread marshmallow cream on his rice cake and then add 15 miniature marshmallows. What a cute, fluffy, and *tasty* tail!

It's Raining! It's Pouring!

Forecast a downpour of learning opportunities with these rain-related centers!

by Mackie Rhodes

by Mackie Rhodes

Rain, Rain

Splash into vocabulary skills with this rainy-day booklet idea. In advance, make a blank booklet for each child by stapling together a copy of the booklet cover (page 31) and several half sheets of paper. Label each of several sentence strips with a different rain-related word and picture as shown. Display the strips at the center. If desired, decorate the center with a raincoat, rubber boots, and a child-safe umbrella. Invite each child to write his name on a booklet cover and then illustrate each rain-related word on a separate page. Challenge him to label each illustration by writing the corresponding word on the page. Encourage him to take his booklet home to share with his family.

Literacy Center

▶ vocabulary development
▶ word recognition
▶ experience with text

Buckets of Raindrops

Dip into estimation and measurement skills with a bucketful of raindrops! Copy the raindrop patterns (page 31) onto blue construction paper to make a supply. Cut the raindrops out and place them in a bucket at the center. Add an assortment of rain gear (hats, boots, umbrella) for the students to measure. Ask a youngster to choose one item and then estimate its length in raindrop patterns. Then have her measure the item using the raindrops. Buckets of fun!

Math Center

▶ measurement skills
▶ nonstandard measurement
▶ estimation

28

Rain Repellent

Little ones will absorb the concept of water repellency with this investigation. In advance, gather an assortment of items for youngsters to test, such as newspaper, fabric squares, vinyl pieces, foam plates, and plastic sandwich bags. Program a chart as shown; then attach a sample of each item to a different column on the chart. Place the chart, test items, a container of blue-tinted water, and several eyedroppers at the center. Before opening the center, discuss the terms *absorb* and *repel* with your class. When a child visits this center, invite her to predict which items will absorb water and which ones will repel water. Then have her investigate by placing a few drops of water onto each item. Encourage her to record her observations on the chart as shown.

Does It Repel Water?					
Name	(newspaper)	(fabric)	(vinyl)	(foam plate)	(plastic bag)
Ashley	☹	☹	☺	☺	☺
Alex					
Jacob	☹	☹	☺	☺	☺
Sophie					

Science Center

observation ◄
predicting outcomes ◄
investigation ◄
vocabulary ◄
development

Muddy Mystery

Mix up some marvelous, mushy mud for a great tactile experience! To prepare, partially fill your sensory table with potting soil. Half-fill a sprinkling can and a bucket with clean water. Gather several plastic items (counters, toys, balls) and several aprons. Then bury the plastic items in the soil so that your students do not see them. Tell your students that there is rainwater in the sprinkling can and bucket and there are mystery objects buried in the soil. Have each child at the center put on an apron. Ask one child to sprinkle the rain onto the soil as others observe. Then have each child use her hands to mix the mud. Encourage her to use only her sense of touch to guess the identity of an object she finds in the mud. Ask her to rinse her item in the bucket of clean water to clear up the muddy mystery.

Sensory Center

tactile investigation ◄
fine-motor skills ◄
observation ◄

▶ fine-motor skills
▶ creativity
▶ color discrimination
▶ hand-eye coordination

Drip, Drip, Drop

Create a shower of colorful raindrops one drip-drop at a time. In advance, cover a table with newspaper. Enlarge and copy the raindrop pattern (page 31) to make a class supply. Use red, blue, and yellow food coloring to tint three separate containers of water. Place the tinted water, three eyedroppers, and the raindrop patterns at the center. Have a child squeeze a dropper of tinted water to allow one droplet at a time to drip onto his pattern. Model how to manipulate the raindrop pattern to roll the droplet back and forth, creating a design. Then have him repeat the process with a different color. Set the raindrops aside to dry. If desired, display the rainbow raindrops for all to enjoy.

Fingerprint Showers

Sprinkle youngsters' creativity across these rainy-day illustrations. To prepare, gather a class supply of white paper, a supply of cotton balls, glue, crayons, and blue paint for the center. Invite each child to use crayons to illustrate an outdoor scene on her paper. Have her glue on cotton ball clouds. Then ask her to create a rain shower by adding blue fingerprints to her scene. Raindrops are falling!

Name ————————————

Raindrop Patterns
Use with "Buckets of Raindrops" on page 28 and "Drip, Drip, Drop" on page 30.

Bugs, Bugs, Bugs!

Explore the world of creepy-crawlies with these buggy centers!

Literacy Center

▶ listening skills
▶ vocabulary development
▶ fine-motor skills

I See a Bug!

Hands down—this active rhyme will be a class favorite. To make a rhyme-telling glove, attach a square of Velcro® to each finger, the thumb, and the palm of a knit glove. Copy, color, and cut out the insect patterns at the bottom of page 35. Then attach the corresponding Velcro square to the back of each pattern. Copy the rhyme below onto chart paper. Then read it aloud to your group as you model how to attach one insect at a time to the glove as shown. Invite each center visitor to use the glove to perform as she recites the rhyme.

Ladybug, ladybug,
What do you see?
I see a firefly blinking by me.
Firefly, firefly,
What do you see?
I see a bumblebee buzzing by me.
Bumblebee, bumblebee,
What do you see?
I see a butterfly fluttering by me.
Butterfly, butterfly,
What do you see?
I see a cricket chirping by me.
Cricket, cricket,
What do you see?
I see a grasshopper jumping on me!

Honeycomb Patterns

Youngsters will buzz around this creative patterning center. In advance, cut two sets of large hexagon shapes from different-colored fabric pieces and place them at the center. If desired, show your students a picture of a real bee's honeycomb and discuss the number of sides on each hexagon-shaped cell. Invite each child to lay the fabric pieces on the floor to create honeycomb designs. Challenge each child to create a pattern with the shapes.

Math Center

▶ patterning
▶ problem solving
▶ creativity

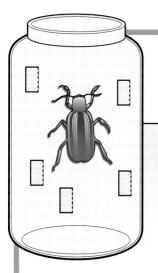

Dramatic-
Play Center

visual discrimination ◄
fine-motor skills ◄
one-to-one ◄
correspondence

Let's Investigate Bugs!

Turn your dramatic-play area into a creepy-crawly investigation station! Enlarge a copy of the bug jar pattern on page 35 onto tagboard. Cut it out and attach several small pieces of Velcro®. Then attach each corresponding piece of Velcro to a plastic insect or an insect sticker. Hide the insects at the center. Gather various bug-hunting tools (a magnifying glass, tongs, hats, nets, insect books) to add to the center. Encourage each child to use the magnifying glass to search for a bug. Have him use the tongs or the net to capture a bug and then attach it to the bug jar. Ask him to count how many bugs he caught; then have him hide them for the next little investigator to find. Hide and seek!

My 👣	
Jacob	5
Sophie	2
Alex	3
Ashley	6

Motor
Center

gross-motor skills ◄
socialization ◄
spatial awareness ◄

Grasshopper Hop!

Youngsters will leap into this active center! Discuss with your students the fact that a grasshopper can jump far—about 20 times the length of its body. Ask them to think about how far they can jump. Set up an area that allows space for one child at a time to jump. Mark the start line by placing a strip of masking tape on the floor. Place a marker (plastic grasshopper or green plastic counter) at the center. Ask a volunteer to model for the class how to stand on the start line, jump one time, and place the marker on the floor. Invite each child to take a turn jumping at the center. Challenge each child to measure the length of his jump by counting the number of footsteps from the start line to his marker. If desired, ask each child to record his findings on a chart as shown.

▶ *fine-motor skills*
▶ *creativity*
▶ *tactile experience*

Busy Bees

Thumbs up! Youngsters' creativity will bloom with these beautiful bee-attracting flowers. In advance, cut out a class supply of tissue paper flowers. Invite a child to place one tissue paper flower on a sheet of white construction paper and then use a paintbrush to cover it with water. She then allows the paper to dry, removes the tissue paper to reveal a flower shape, and uses crayons to add a stem and leaves. To make bees, have her use yellow paint to make several thumbprints on her paper; let it dry. Then use a black marker to add features to each bee as shown.

▶ *tactile experience*
▶ *fine-motor skills*
▶ *tactile discrimination*

My bug is soft and bumpy.

Bumpy Bugs

Touchable bugs! Youngsters will enjoy creating their own feely-bugs with this tactile activity. In advance, cut out a class supply of bug body shapes, each from the center of a 9" x 12" sheet of construction paper. Place them at the center along with a class supply of 9" x 12" sheets of construction paper, wiggle eyes, and a variety of textured materials (cotton balls, aluminum foil, feathers, etc.). Have each child glue textured materials onto a full sheet of construction paper and then glue the bug cutout sheet on top of it. Encourage her to decorate her bug as desired. Later, have her dictate a descriptive sentence about her bug as you write it on her paper.

Insect Patterns
Use with "I See a Bug!" on page 32.

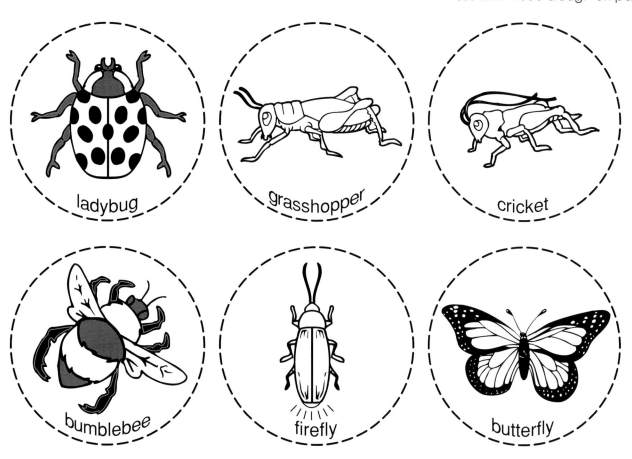

ladybug

grasshopper

cricket

bumblebee

firefly

butterfly

Dandelion Delights

Delight your little learners with this collection of dandy center activities.

by Mackie Rhodes

Literacy Center

▶ fine-motor skills
▶ writing skills
▶ letter recognition

Dandy Pencil Pointers

Fluff up your little ones' literacy skills with these dandelion pencils that double as pointers. To begin, invert a Styrofoam® cup and glue Easter grass all over it to resemble a grassy mound. For each pencil pointer that you'd like to make, trace a milk jug lid two times on white or yellow felt. Cut out the circle; then fringe-cut along the edges. Hot-glue a cutout to each side of the eraser of a sharpened green pencil. Poke several of these dandelion pencils into the grassy mound. Place the dandelion mound in a center along with a supply of paper and children's books. Encourage students to use the pencils to practice writing *D*s, drawing pictures of things that begin with *D,* and pointing to *D*s in books. How "*D*-lightful"!

Math Center

▶ number recognition
▶ counting
▶ fine-motor skills

A Dandy Spinner

Math skills are growing like weeds at this center! Copy the leaf and circle patterns (page 39) on construction paper as indicated. Cut out each pattern; then label the circle with a number in each section (as appropriate for your students). To make a large dandelion, glue the circle to a small paper plate. Poke a hole in the center; then fringe-cut the plate rim. Cover a potato chip canister with green paper. Attach the dandelion to the canister with a paper fastener. Glue each leaf to a craft stick; then hot-glue the leaves to the canister as shown. Use a green marker to draw an arrow stem between the leaves. Fill the canister with white pom-poms and snap on the lid. To do this activity, a child empties the canister of pom-poms. Then he spins the dandelion to see which number the arrow stem will point to. Next, he counts out that many pom-poms and puts them in the canister. Have the child keep spinning and counting until all the pom-poms are back in the canister.

Seeds in the Breeze

Exploring seed travel is a breeze with this idea! To make dandelion seeds, cut a supply of three-inch white tissue paper squares. Twist the center of each square into a point as shown to resemble a dandelion seed. Fluff out the tops of some of the seeds and tightly twist the tops of the others. Poke the eraser end of a green pencil into a Styrofoam® ball. Use the dull end of another pencil to poke holes all around the ball. Place the "bald" dandelion in your science center along with the seeds. Invite each visitor to carefully insert the seeds into the dandelion. Then have him blow on it. What happens? Why do some seeds fly off? Why do some seeds stay put? The winds of discovery are blowing!

Science Center

observation ◄
investigation ◄
analytical thinking ◄

Dandelion Garden

Turn your sand table into a yellow and white garden delight! To prepare, gather a supply of green craft sticks and yellow and white pom-poms. Hot-glue each pom-pom to a craft stick to resemble either a yellow dandelion flower or a white dandelion puff. Spray the sand in your sand table with water to make it moist. Add the dandelions and an assortment of child-safe garden tools to the sand. For this activity, each child shapes a garden in the sand. Then she plants the dandelions as desired—in straight rows of color, alternating patterns, shapes, or even letters! What a dandy garden!

Sensory Center

sensory experience ◄
spatial awareness ◄
fine-motor skills ◄

Art Center

▶ *fine-motor skills*
▶ *following directions*
▶ *creative expression*

Personal Puffs

There's a lot of valuable cutting practice in this project! To begin, have each center visitor trace the bottom of a paper cup on white paper four or five times. Then have him cut out each circle and glue them all together *only at the centers.* Next, have the child fringe-cut all around the stacked circles. Then direct him to glue the fringed circle to a green craft stick. If desired, invite him to glue on green construction paper leaves and then fluff the fringes to make a puff.

Cooking Center

▶ *fine-motor skills*
▶ *following directions*
▶ *creative expression*

Delicious Dandelions

This nutritious dandelion is sure to tickle your little ones' tummies! To make one, have the child spread softened cream cheese on a round cracker. Then encourage her to sprinkle on grated cheddar cheese to resemble a dandelion flower. Or, if she prefers, she can make a white dandelion puff by sprinkling on grated Swiss cheese. Mmm, just dandy!

circle

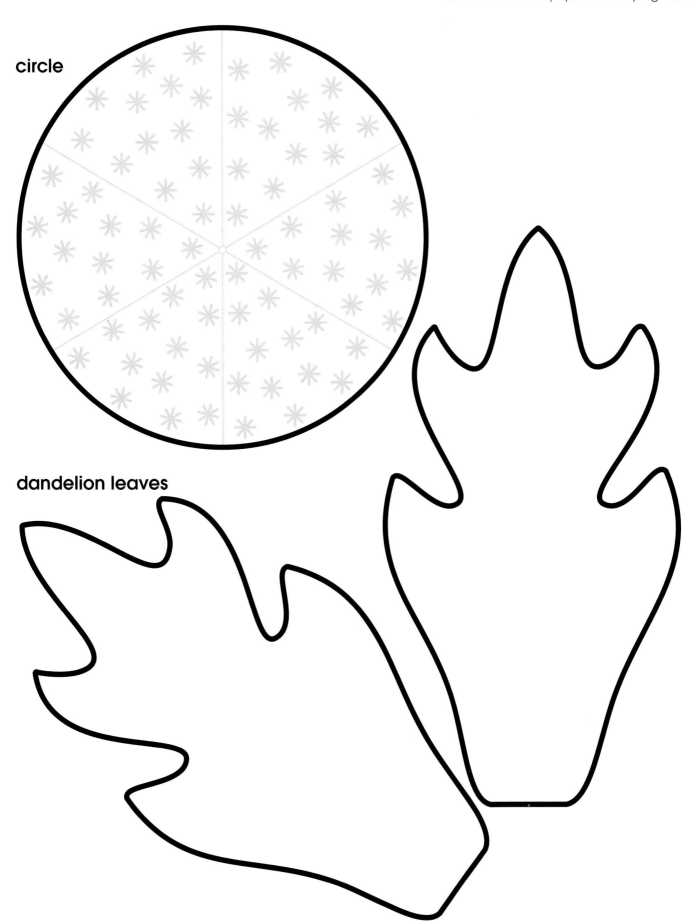

dandelion leaves

The Garden

*It's time to plant these seeds
of learning in your classroom
garden!*

by Suzanne Moore

Sandy Writing

**Literacy
Center**

▶ *fine-motor skills*
▶ *left-to-right
progression*
▶ *writing skills*

Rev up each of your little sprouts' writing skills with this ready-to-go center. Pour sand into a few plastic window boxes (or plastic shoeboxes) and place them in your literacy center along with "writing tools," such as a plastic trowel, a plastic knife, and an unsharpened pencil. Display alphabet letters, color and number words, and vocabulary words nearby. Encourage youngsters to settle down with a writing box and a writing tool and write words and letters in the sand. Their writing skills will surely grow!

Flower Power Patterning

**Math
Center**

▶ *patterning*
▶ *fine-motor skills*
▶ *creative expression*

Patterning practice has never been prettier! First, prepare a few homemade stamp pads by pouring different colors of paint into Styrofoam® trays lined with paper towels. Provide strips of art paper and flower-shaped sponges (or cut your own shapes from sponges with a craft knife). Encourage each child who visits this center to use the supplies to sponge-paint her own original patterns. When the paint is dry, invite children to describe their flower patterns during circle time.

Bird in the Garden

Little ones will love this cube puzzle game focusing on a legendary garden lover: a bird! In advance, wrap an empty tissue cube with paper. Next, reproduce the puzzle patterns (page 43) four times. Color, laminate, and cut apart all of the puzzle sets. Glue each piece of the fourth set to a different panel on the tissue box cube. To play this game, give one to three players a set of puzzle pieces. Have the first player roll the cube and find the puzzle piece from his set that matches the one on the top of the cube. He puts that piece in place to assemble his puzzle. If a player rolls a piece that he already has in place, continue play with the next player. The first person to complete his puzzle is the early bird!

Manipulatives Center

visual discrimination ◄
spatial awareness ◄

Garden Patch Visor

Youngsters will enjoy creating and wearing this visor that's just perfect for gardening! In advance, cut a class supply of nine-inch paper plates as shown in the illustration. Place the cut visors in your art center along with a supply of glue, silk flowers (stems removed), glitter crayons, construction paper scraps, ribbons, bows, and markers. Invite each child to decorate a visor as she wishes. When she's done decorating, loop two rubber bands together; then help her staple the looped bands to each end of the visor to get a perfect fit.

Art Center

fine-motor skills ◄
water exploration ◄
hand-eye ◄
coordination

"Kinder-garden"

Set up this garden center in a corner of your classroom and your little ones will be busy, busy in the garden! Pour a layer of potting soil or sand in a child's plastic swimming pool. Put it in a corner of your room. Then set up white picket fence garden edging along the walls. Add toy gardening tools; straw hats; and plastic fruits, veggies, and flowers. Include a few baskets so your gardening buffs can gather some of their own garden goodies.

Dramatic-Play Center

▶ creative thinking
▶ role-playing
▶ verbal skills

Watering Day

A garden can't survive without water, and your water table is the perfect place for youngsters to practice the skills of not-too-much and not-too-little. Put a variety of watering cans in your water-filled table. Also add an assortment of waterproof toys—flowers, fruits, and vegetables would be perfect! Encourage children to explore using the different types of watering cans and trying to pour just the right amount of water over the toys.

Sensory Center

▶ gross-motor skills
▶ creative play

Beautiful Butterflies

Flitter, flutter—your youngsters will glide through this collection of butterfly-related activities!

by Susan DeRiso

Literacy Center

▶ *vocabulary development*
▶ *sequencing*
▶ *experience with text*

Puzzle Poems

Piece together a poetic connection with this creative puzzle. To prepare, trace a large butterfly pattern onto a colorful sheet of tagboard. Cut it out and then cut it into three sections as shown. Write one line from the poem on each section as shown. Then lay the butterfly on a table and mix up the pieces. Read aloud the poem to your class. Ask each child at the center to sequence the lines of the poem, creating the butterfly shape. For a more challenging activity, ask youngsters to help create a poem to write on the butterfly.

Butterfly, way up high,

Flying in the clear blue sky,

Waving with a wing, "Good-bye!"

Math Center

▶ *matching*
▶ *symmetry*
▶ *visual discrimination*

Symmetrical Patterns

Equally amazing! Youngsters will learn about symmetry as they match up this beautiful pattern-block butterfly. Make a class supply of the butterfly pattern on page 47 and place the patterns at a center along with a supply of pattern blocks. Invite each child to use a block to cover each corresponding shape on the butterfly. Encourage her to compare the butterfly wings, noticing they are exactly the same design and color. If desired, have her remove one block at a time and color each shape on her butterfly.

Butterfly Life Cycle

Youngsters will love the "pasta-bilities" of creating this model of the butterfly life cycle. Discuss with your students the stages of metamorphosis from a caterpillar to a butterfly. If desired, display books or pictures of the butterfly life cycle. Stock your center with a class supply of 2" x 8" tagboard strips and the following pasta types in various colors: orzo, spirals, shells, and bow ties. You may want to program each strip with the words "egg," "caterpillar," "chrysalis," and "butterfly." Invite each child to glue pasta onto his strip (and draw on details) to create the butterfly life cycle as shown.

Science Center

sequencing ◄
fine-motor skills ◄

egg   caterpillar   chrysalis   butterfly

Fluttering Surprise

Pop, pop, pop! Crack the chrysalis to reveal a beautiful butterfly. Gather a class supply of short paper tubes and plastic straws. Prepare each tube by taping a 3" circle of brown paper to cover one end. If desired, have each child color or paint the paper tube brown or green to represent the chrysalis. Then make a 3" butterfly tracer by drawing a simple butterfly shape onto tagboard. Ask the student to trace the butterfly shape onto white paper, decorate it, and cut it out. Tape the butterfly onto the end of a straw. Gently curl the butterfly wings inward and insert the straw into the open end of the chrysalis, butterfly end first. Encourage the student to explain the butterfly life cycle as he pushes the straw to help his butterfly emerge from its chrysalis.

Art Center

hand-eye ◄
coordination
following directions ◄
fine-motor skills ◄

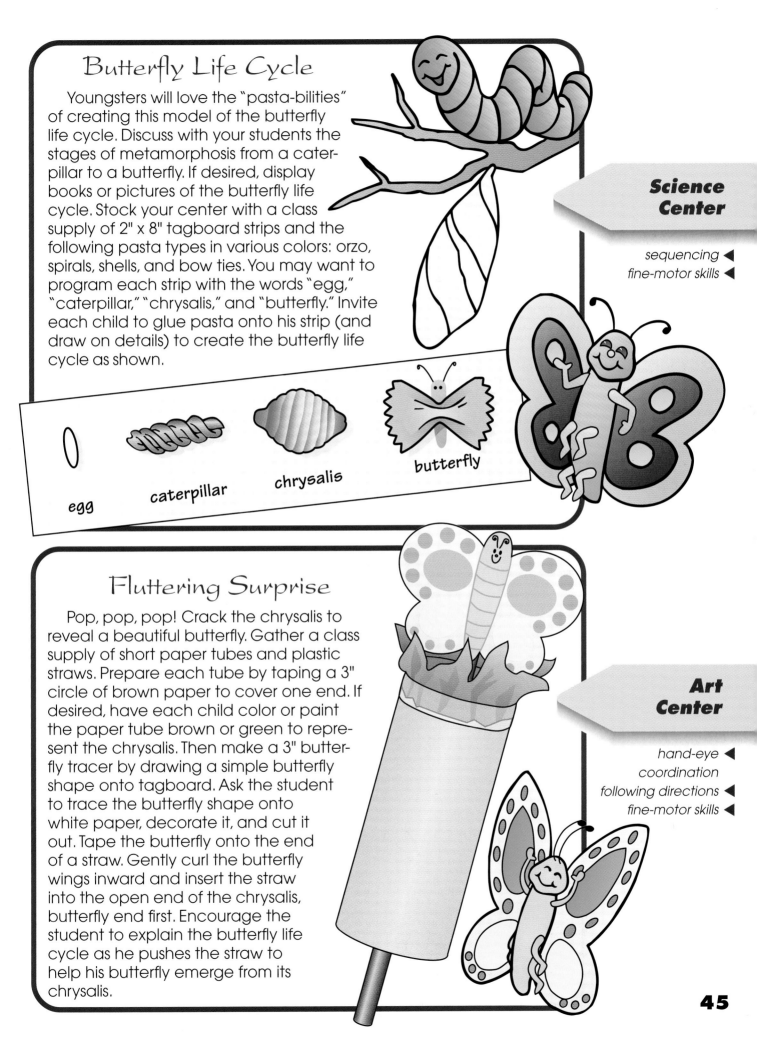

Caterpillar Necklace

Improve fine-motor skills with these tasty caterpillar necklaces. In advance, gather a class supply of string licorice and fruit-flavored cereal loops (large and small sizes). Prepare each necklace by tying one cereal loop on one end as shown. Encourage each child to create a caterpillar by stringing cereal loops onto her necklace. If desired, have her reproduce a pattern you have specified. Then tie the ends together to make a wiggly necklace.

Motor Center

▶ fine-motor skills
▶ sensory experience
▶ color recognition
▶ patterning

Butterfly Snacks

This healthy snack is almost too cute to eat! To prepare, gather apples (half per child), bananas (quarter per child), raisins, shredded cheese, peanut butter, bowls, and a class supply of plastic spoons. Remove the seeds from the apple halves and place them in a bowl of water mixed with one tablespoon of lemon juice. Place the other supplies in individual bowls at the center. Have each child use his spoon to spread peanut butter onto an apple and then place the banana in the center of it. Ask him to use peanut butter to add raisin eyes and cheese antennas. Decorate the butterfly wings as desired with raisins or cheese. Yum!

Cooking Center

▶ following directions
▶ fine-motor skills
▶ tactile experience

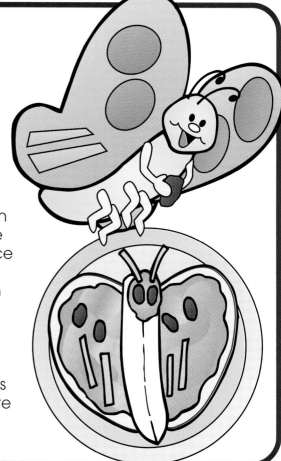

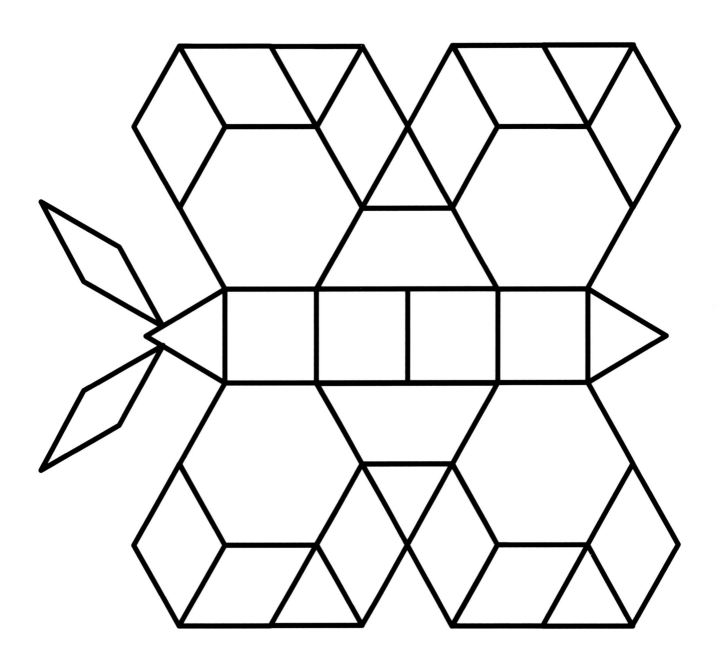

Gators Galore!

Snap, snap! These alligator-themed centers are swamped with great learning skills.

by Mackie Rhodes

Literacy Center

▶ letter recognition
▶ identifying letter sounds
▶ phonemic awareness

Alligator Eggs

Hatch a batch of literacy skills with this "eggs-ceptional" idea! To prepare, make three green construction paper copies of the alligator pattern (page 51). Cut out the patterns and then decorate them as desired. Next, gather three plastic eggs, three paper bowls, magnetic letters, a magnetic dry-erase board, and dry-erase markers. Staple an alligator pattern on the bottom of each bowl. Seal a different letter in each egg; then cover each egg with an alligator bowl. To do this activity, invite a child to catch an alligator, open its egg, and remove the letter. Ask her to name the letter and the letter sound. Have her place the letter on the magnetic board and then draw a picture of something that begins with that letter sound. Encourage her to repeat the process with the remaining alligators and then return the letters to the eggs. (Periodically change the letters that are hidden inside the eggs.)

bear

Math Center

▶ nonstandard measurement
▶ counting
▶ problem solving

Gator Measurement

Chomp into measurement skills with these crafty gators! To make one gator, hot-glue wiggle eyes and two bumpy chenille stem legs to a large green craft stick and add details as shown. (You will need to make two gators for each child at the center.) Invite each child to measure objects in the classroom using the gator sticks. Have him draw each object on a sheet of paper and record its length in gator sticks. If desired, have pairs of students work together to measure and record.

Alligator's Lunch

Help the gators sort out their favorite lunches! In advance, make six copies of page 51 and cut out one set of food labels and the six alligator patterns. Glue one label on each alligator and decorate as desired. Then attach each alligator to a separate empty box. Place the alligator boxes and an assortment of plastic foods, empty food containers, or pictures of foods at the center. Include several different foods from each food group. Ask a child to sort the foods by type and place each one in the appropriately labeled box. Snip, snap, sort!

Science Center

sorting ◀
visual ◀
discrimination
matching ◀

Swamp Gators

Youngsters will glide through this swamp full of sinking and floating exploration. In advance, make a supply of the alligators from "Gator Measurement" on page 48. To create a swamp, partially fill your sensory table with clean aquarium gravel, pour in blue-tinted water, and add Easter grass. Gather several different items for float/sink experimentation, such as crayons, blocks, plastic counters, rocks, and small plastic toys. Invite a child to explore the swamp by helping a gator swim, dive, and float in it. Have him choose one item, predict if it will sink or float, and then place it in the swamp. Encourage him to manipulate his gator to dive or swim to retrieve the item.

Sensory Center

floating and sinking ◀
prediction ◀
sensory ◀

Home, Home in the Swamp

Set youngsters' imaginations in motion when they don an alligator cap and explore this swampy habitat. To make one cap, enlarge a copy of the alligator pattern (page 51) and trace it onto a sheet of craft foam. Cut out the pattern, glue on wiggle eyes, and decorate it as desired. Then staple it onto the bottom of a dust mask as shown. Place several alligator caps, plastic eggs, an assortment of plastic water animals, and a large box filled with brown crinkle strips (for a gator nest) at the center. Invite several children to put on caps and pretend they are great gators gliding through the swamp.

Grainy Green Gators

Please pet the alligators! Youngsters will create bumpy-textured gators that beg to be touched. To make one tactile gator, cut out a green construction paper copy of the alligator pattern (page 51). Spread glue on the gator and sprinkle it with uncooked rice. Then squeeze more glue over the rice and firmly press a 6" x 12" piece of green tissue paper on top of it. Add wiggle eyes and let dry. Then trim the excess tissue paper to shape the gator.

Art Center

▶ fine-motor skills
▶ hand-eye coordination
▶ tactile experience

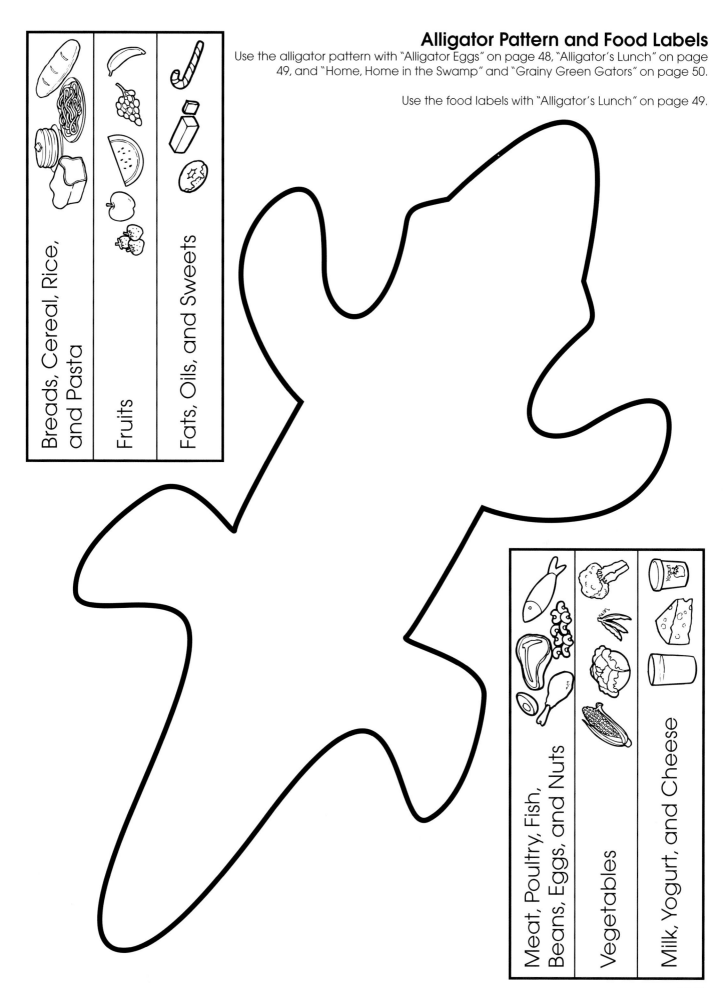

Alligator Pattern and Food Labels

Use the alligator pattern with "Alligator Eggs" on page 48, "Alligator's Lunch" on page 49, and "Home, Home in the Swamp" and "Grainy Green Gators" on page 50.

Use the food labels with "Alligator's Lunch" on page 49.

Breads, Cereal, Rice, and Pasta

Fruits

Fats, Oils, and Sweets

Meat, Poultry, Fish, Beans, Eggs, and Nuts

Vegetables

Milk, Yogurt, and Cheese

Squiggly, Wiggly Worms!

Mud, worms, and kids just seem to go together to create all kinds of learning fun!

by Valerie R. Corbeille

blue   A B C   John

Literacy Center

▶ *left-to-right progression*
▶ *fine-motor skills*
▶ *visual discrimination*

Wormy Words

Words are crawling all over the place at this center! In advance, cook spaghetti according to the package directions and rinse it well. (To color the noodles, add a few drops of food coloring to the water when you cook them.) Drain the colored noodles; then store them in a sealed bowl. To set up the center, arrange the noodles and a supply of sentence strips in view of your classroom alphabet chart or word wall. When children visit this center, encourage them to arrange the spaghetti on a sentence strip to form letters, words, or their names. The spaghetti will stick to the paper without glue because of the starch in the pasta. Especially good for your tactile learners!

Wiggle Worms

Counting and fine-motor skills combine to make these wiggly worms an educational delight! Stock your motor center with a supply of pipe cleaner halves and small beads. Have each child choose a pipe cleaner half and then string ten beads onto it. Show him how to turn the pipe cleaner ends over the last bead on each end to prevent slipping. With a small group, use a collection of ten of these worms to practice counting to 100 by tens. Afterward, these wiggly worms can wrap around pencils, desk legs, fingers, or just about anywhere!

Motor Center

▶ *fine-motor skills*
▶ *counting*
▶ *skip-counting*

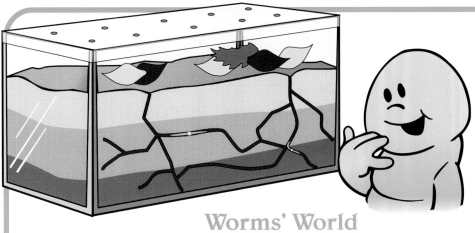

Worms' World

Well…you might as well face it. You're going to need some of those slimy critters in your classroom! Enlist the help of your students to create a worm habitat in an aquarium (or large-mouth glass jar). Pour alternate layers of damp soil and sand in the aquarium. Place several worms on the soil; then lightly cover the soil with decaying leaves. Cover the top of the aquarium with plastic wrap; then punch holes in the wrap. Tape black paper around all the sides. Let the worms' world sit undisturbed for several days. Then remove the coverings and position the aquarium in a shaded spot in your science center with paper, pencils, crayons, and magnifying lenses. (Be sure to add leaves when necessary and keep the soil slightly moist.) Invite children to visit this center, examine the habitat, and record their findings. How has the habitat changed? Do the worms seem to notice you? How can you tell? Would you like to gently hold a worm? What happens when you touch it?

The Worm Walk

Your youngsters may not cover much distance, but they'll have a great time trying out the worm walk! In advance, demonstrate how to do the worm walk. Stand with your feet together. Then bend and touch your hands to the floor. Walk your hands forward without moving your feet. Then walk your feet up to your hands. Repeat the process. When children come to this center, invite them to do the worm walk or lie on the floor and wiggle like a worm in their own way. If desired, set up a cardboard tunnel and invite your little worms to wiggle their way through it. This worm walk gets the wiggles out!

Working Worms

Industrious imaginations will work hard in this center! Fill a sensory tub with slightly moist potting soil. Add several rubber worms to the soil along with silk flowers, spoons for planting, and an empty watering can. When a child visits this center, encourage him to use the worms to aerate the soil. Then invite him to design a flourishing garden in the aerated soil.

Cooking Center

▶ following directions
▶ left-to-right progression
▶ fine-motor skills

Wiggle Worm Parfait

This parfait is not for the faint of heart! For this activity you will need enough chocolate pudding for each child to have about a half cup, crushed chocolate cookies, one or two Gummy worms per child, plastic spoons, and clear plastic tumblers. To prepare the center, photocopy the recipe cards (page 55). Color and cut apart the cards; then laminate them. Display them in sequence in your cooking center. Then arrange the ingredients and supplies for easy student access. Invite each child to come to the center and make a wiggle worm parfait.

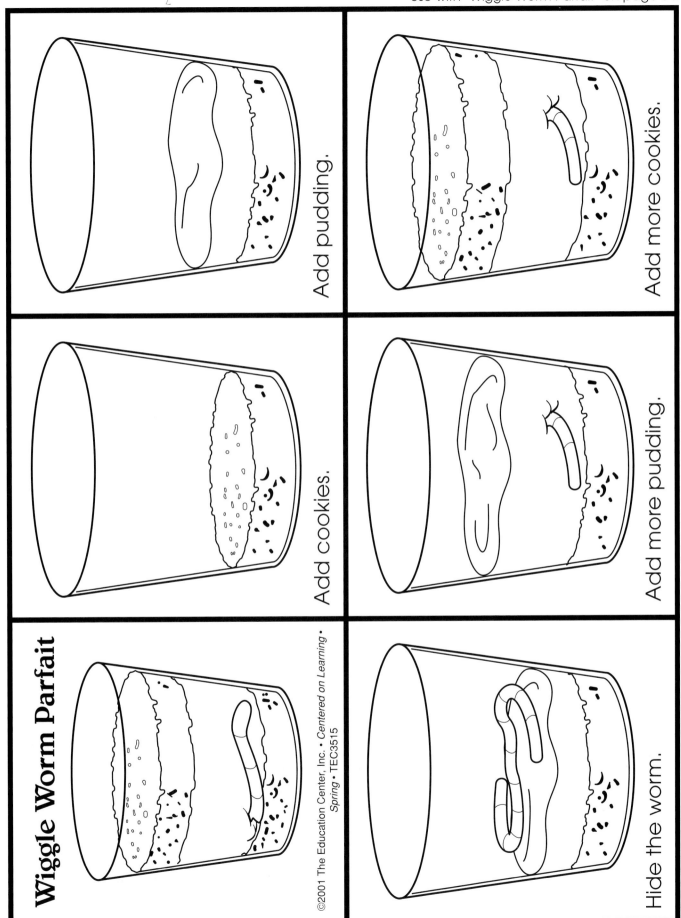

Add pudding.

Add more cookies.

Add cookies.

Add more pudding.

Wiggle Worm Parfait

Hide the worm.

Pets

Unleash the fun of creative learning with these playful pet centers!

by Sandra Faulkner

Fine-Motor Center

▶ classification
▶ vocabulary development

Pocketful of Pets

Strengthen classification skills with this center. For this activity, you'll need two paper plate pockets. To make one, cut one paper plate in half. Align the front of a paper plate half along the edge of a separate whole plate. Hole-punch along the edges through both plates. Then use yarn to lace the plates together, creating a pocket. Label one plate "Pets" and the other "Not Pets."

Next, cut out a large variety of animal pictures from magazines. Glue each picture to a different index card. To do this activity, have a child look at each animal card and then place it in the appropriate pocket. Some of the animals might require a little extra discussion—according to your youngsters!

Tricks With Treats

Children will do all sorts of educational tricks with these treats! To prepare, fill a clean dog bowl with a variety of dog treats. When a child visits this center, encourage her to sort the treats by color, type, size, or any other attribute. If desired, encourage the child to use the treats to make a pattern, too. Good student!

Manipulatives Center

▶ sorting
▶ patterning

Pet Vet

Here's a chance to doctor up some creative thinking as well as lots of other skills! Stock your dramatic-play center with a variety of stuffed animals, gauze, cotton balls, stretch bandages, and cloth bandaging material. Also add notepads, pencils, and an appointment book. Invite children who visit this center to set up a veterinarian's office. Encourage them to play the roles of veterinarian, assistant, office staff, and clients. Make no bones about it—this is dramatic play at its best!

Dramatic-Play Center

creative thinking ◄
role-playing ◄
socialization ◄
writing ◄

Block Center

fine-motor skills ◄
creative thinking ◄
spatial awareness ◄

A House for Me!

Architectural skills are front and center for this home-building activity! To begin, arrange of variety of different toy animals in your block center. Encourage each child who visits this center to design a house, pen, or crate for each of the different animals. Not too big. Not too small. Ah, this one is just right!

Literacy Center

▶ *writing*
▶ *creative thinking*
▶ *socialization*

"Paws-itive" Notes

Here's a pet-related twist to add to your writing center. Provide pawprint rubber stamps and stamp pads. (If you don't have rubber stamps that are appropriate for this, make a pawprint potato printer and have children use it with tempera paint.) In the center, also include pencils with pet designs or pet-related pencil toppers. Set the tone for the center by adding pet-related books or even your live classroom pet. Encourage children to visit the center both to design stationery for general use and to write letters to classmates, school staff members, or people in their families.

Here, Doggie!

This little puppy is begging to help with math skills! In advance, make ten construction paper copies of the puppy and bone patterns (page 59). Color, cut out, and laminate the patterns. Using a permanent marker, write a different number on each puppy's tag. For each number, draw a corresponding dot set on a bone. To do this activity, have a child match each bone to a puppy. For variety, provide a supply of real dog biscuits and ask a student to give each dog the corresponding number of biscuits.

Math Center

▶ *number recognition*
▶ *counting*

puppy

bone

COME TO THE CIRCUS!

Ladies and gentlemen! Step right up to these extraordinary circus centers that provide cross-curricular learning fun for one and all!

by Mackie Rhodes

CLOWNING AROUND WITH SOUNDS

Get into the act with this funny phonics clown. To make a clown, copy, color, and cut out the clown face and letter strip (page 64). Label each section of the letter strip with a letter that your class is currently studying. Glue the face to the center of a paper plate. Add hair, a hat, and other clown features as desired. Cut slits on the clown where indicated and then slide the letter strip through them as shown. Put the clown in a center with several circus books. To do this activity, have a child pull the letter strip to display a letter in the clown's smile. Then encourage him to search the books to find characters, pictures, or words beginning with that letter's sound. Have him repeat the process with the other letters on the strip. Come join the act!

CIRCUS SNACKS

A circus is just not complete without those yummy circus treats! Collect empty containers from candy, animal crackers, soda, and juice. Fill zippered plastic bags with circus-related toy foods, such as hot dogs, hamburgers, and pizza. Put real popcorn, peanuts, and pretzels in small resealable bags. Then label each item with a price (within your students' abilities). Put the foods in a center with trays, wallets, paper money, and a toy cash register. For this activity, encourage students to set up a concession stand and then use the provided materials to role-play concession attendants and customers. Step right up for the greatest snacks on earth!

Hot Dog
10¢

FEEDING TIME

Feeding time is a balancing act at this circus! Put a balance scale, a bucket of dried beans (for animal feed), scoops or spoons, a supply of clear plastic tumblers, and pairs of toy circus animals in a center. Then invite each visitor to feed the animals. For each pair of animals, the child scoops some feed into a tumbler. She puts the filled tumbler on one side of the scale and an empty one on the opposite side. Then she estimates how much feed to add to the empty tumbler in order to balance the scale. Too much? Take a little out. Too little? Add some more. When both containers hold the same amount of feed, she gives one to each of her hungry twosome. Start scooping—these guys are hungry!

POPCORN AND PEANUTS

This idea is a circus "sense-sation"! In advance, request that each family send in a bag of plain popped popcorn or a bag of peanuts in the shells. Mix the snacks in your sensory tub. Add scoops, bowls, and small paper bags labeled "Peanuts and Popcorn." (Tell students that this mixture is not for eating.) When a child visits this center, encourage him to experience the many sensations provided by this mixture—the contrasting colors and shapes, the sounds of scooping and pouring, and the odors and textures of the two snacks. At snacktime, add taste to the sensations with a fresh batch of peanuts and popcorn!

61

ANIMAL-CRACKER ART

Here's a fun and easy craft that's right in step with your circus unit. Give each child several animal crackers (the circus variety) to glue onto a piece of white art paper. Ask her to imagine a circus scene around her crackers. Then provide her with crayons, markers, and assorted art supplies and encourage her to create her imagined scene on the paper. For the big finish, of course, offer a fresh batch of animal crackers for snacking!

AFTER THE SHOW

Caring for the animals after a busy day at the circus can be quite a chore! In your block center, provide a collection of toy circus animals, brushes, washcloths, a bar of soap, a small broom, and plastic bowls. Also add a bucket of dried beans (animal feed) and spoons or small scoops. Invite each visitor to imagine that he is the animal caretaker for a circus. Ask him to arrange the blocks to create pens for the animals. Then have him perform caretaking duties for the animals, such as grooming, feeding, and cleaning up after them. Whew! So much work to be done!

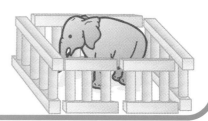

MY RED BALLOON

What's a circus without balloons? For this singing activity, you'll need a laminated red balloon cutout for each child in the center. In advance, sing the song below several times into a tape recorder, substituting a different position for the balloon each time. Then announce (on the tape) that you're going to continue singing the song, leaving a blank in the place of each position word or phrase. Encourage the listeners to fill in their own ideas. Put the tape and the balloons in your music area. Encourage each center visitor to listen to the song and move his balloon appropriately. After the first few verses, watch for the *original* song and dance to begin!

MY RED BALLOON

(sung to the tune of "He's Got the Whole World in His Hands")

I've got my red balloon (<u>over my head</u>).
I've got my red balloon (<u>over my head</u>).
I've got my red balloon (<u>over my head</u>).
I've got my red balloon (<u>over my head</u>).

I've got my red balloon (<u>behind my knees</u>)...
I've got my red balloon (<u>out to the right</u>)...
I've got my red balloon (<u>on my elbow</u>)...

Music and Movement Center

gross-motor skills ◄
position words ◄
creative thinking ◄

CIRCUS PARADE

Here's a parade of circus animals that's also a tasty treat! To make a parade, have two or more children visit this center together. Instruct each child to spread a generous amount of creamy peanut butter on the top of several vanilla wafers. Then have each child press an animal cracker into the peanut butter on each wafer. Encourage the children to set up their parade on napkins or paper towels. After admiring their parade, it's time to eat!

Cooking Center

fine-motor skills ◄
following directions ◄

Patterns

Use with "Clowning Around With Sounds" on page 60.

clown face

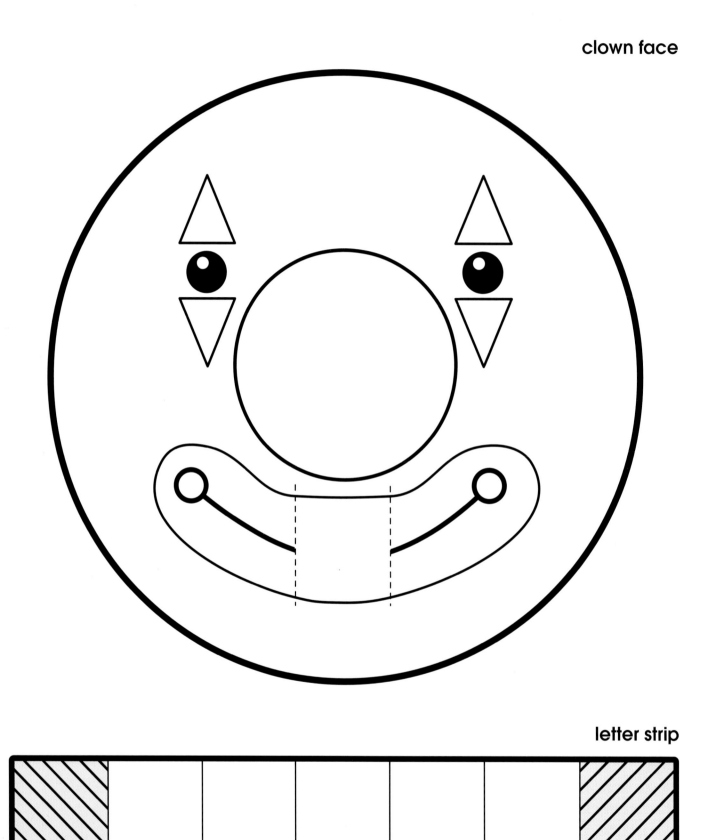

letter strip